T0128948

OPTION TRADE LIKE
VICTORIA

MY OPTION TO TRADE OPTION
Stressless Living with Option Trade —Surefire Income Generator

Victoria C. Okonkwo, BA, M.Ed, R.N.

authorHOUSE®

AuthorHouse™
1663 Liberty Drive
Bloomington, IN 47403
www.authorhouse.com
Phone: 1 (800) 839-8640

© 2018 Victoria C. Okonkwo, BA, M.Ed, R.N. All rights reserved.

No part of this book may be reproduced, stored in a retrieval system, or transmitted by any means without the written permission of the author.

Published by AuthorHouse 01/04/2018

ISBN: 978-1-5462-2148-7 (sc)
ISBN: 978-1-5462-2147-0 (e)

Print information available on the last page.

Any people depicted in stock imagery provided by Thinkstock are models, and such images are being used for illustrative purposes only. Certain stock imagery © Thinkstock.

This book is printed on acid-free paper.

Because of the dynamic nature of the Internet, any web addresses or links contained in this book may have changed since publication and may no longer be valid. The views expressed in this work are solely those of the author and do not necessarily reflect the views of the publisher, and the publisher hereby disclaims any responsibility for them.

CONTENTS

CHAPTER 1

WELCOME TO OPTIONS PLATFORM

Victoria creates a hub and invites the unemployed, the frustrated, retired nurses, stay home moms and pops, and other everyday individuals interested in discovering new avenues for generating part or fulltime income. This book is informative, inspiring, sure fire income generator!

Are you looking for a career change? Are you unemployed, or under-employed? Are you frustrated, given up, and have fallen out of the band-wagon of job applicants? How long ago have you been able to carve out enough money at the end of the month to pay for your mortgage, rent, and other bills conveniently, and on time. Have you been able to carve out enough money at the end of the month to pay for your mortgage, rent, and other important bills with your laptop connected to the internet? You probably have never imagined that you can connect your laptop to the internet and make money to pay your bills. Yes, you can! Stocks and Options trading online have endless possibilities.

Sounds too good to be true? It is true! Some skeptics who have no idea will quickly say "No Way."

I hereby refute their negativity, and unequivocally state—"Yes Way." Speaking from personal experience, I reiterate, 'Yes way' "Yes you Can!" You can trade "Stocks & Options online for a living." Since 2012, I cut down on my full–time nursing job, and have been able to sustain myself, pay my mortgage, and pay my bills from my Stock/Options trading business income, especially when the market is booming—"the Bull Market."

WHY TRADE STOCKS AND OPTIONS ONLINE?

Freedom is the allure of my option to trade stocks and options online. I sit in my home office, with my laptop and internet connection, and carve out my living from the stocks and options market.

You will have the freedom to be your own boss! You can work when you want, where you want, and trade what you want, and be on your way to financial independence. How? Information is power, especially in this modern age when every human living is digitalized. The information in this book will help the unemployed looking for job, nurses burnt out from long standing hours at work, housewives wanting to work at home, retired nurses who are not sure what alternative source of income is out there. If you are not sure what, how, where, or when to start exploring other avenues for extra income, this book will help you out. Having a bird's eye view on the meaning of stocks/options, the history of stocks/options, the strategies used in trading options, and the advantages of one over the other will help you to widen your horizon on the knowledge of Stock vs Option trade. Knowing the difference will remove the misunderstandings which are verbalized by some skeptics about stocks/options. Each new thing learned and mastered in this book is a new reason for loving options trade and believing in it. This book will progressively be concerned with options trade as the guaranteed means to create wealth, decrease loss, and lead you to financial freedom. Some say that stock is good, better than option, that option is risky and will wipe you out. Some say that option is the best means to financial freedom. In this book, Victoria gives a brief discussion on the history of stocks in the ancient and modern world; the differences between stocks and options with reference to what they are, the trading education required, strategies, and their trading characteristics.

To begin trading stocks and options online you need to learn the tricks of the trade, and learn the ropes. You should have access to various sources of very good stocks and options trading education, strategies, strong trading skills-set, and personal style.

You need a Laptop, Internet Connection for the electronic trading.

CHAPTER 2

PREPARATORY REQUIREMENTS

Education

Option trading is not stock trading. It is a good thing and highly recommended to be an educated option trader before you plunge head on into trading. If you have the required option education and the trading skills, you can learn, design, and apply option strategies that will help you profit from a wide variety of stock market outcomes with little risk. You can accomplish this with little risk if you have the required education and options trading skills.

Experience and Training

My thanks go to the trading schools like: Options Made Easy, Online Trading Academy, and The Better Trades Team who made options education available to me at the onset of my quest for option trading education. They prepared me for online stocks and options trading.

CNBC

I watch CNBC! The daily Booyah, (Mad Money with Jim Cramer). Thanks also to the team members of the Squawk Team: The twin brothers: Pete and Jon Najarian for their book "How We Trade Options" (Building Wealth, Creating Income, and Reducing Risk); Jim Cramer for his book: "Get Rich.?" Watch America's post-market show "Fast Money" and "Options Actions." These shows are hosted by Emmy-nominated Melissa Lee. "Fast Money" brings important actionable news to investors during the day. Panelist include: Guy Adami (Chief Market Strategist & Director of Advisor Advocacy, Private Advisor Group); Karen Finerman (CEO & Co-founder, Metropolitan Capital Advisors); Steve Grasso (Director of Institutional Sales Stuart Frankel & Co. Inc.); Brian Kelly (Founder & Managing Member, Kelly Capital LLC). Experienced option traders from top firms on wall street make up the panel of "Options Action." Panelist include: Michael Khouw, Dan Nathan, and Carter Braxton Worth. Their weekly fast paced, half-hour show focuses on measures to maximize profits and limit losses while applying the common option techniques.

No Education is wasted!

If you have financial help it is advisable to go to a trading school, take courses to learn and study the tricks of the trade, to get qualified and arm yourself with a formal trading certificate.

Arm yourself with Online Stock and Option trading education. Attend several trading seminars and webinars. You can also get more options education help from the education department of the Options Industry Council (OIC). Call 18886784667 to chat with support team, or visit their website at www.optionseducation.org for any questions you have about trading options. You can also have access to educational materials like articles, research papers, live seminars, videos, free option classes. OIC is a department in the US options exchanges and the Options Clearing Corporation (OCC). Other helpful sites for options education on articles stock news include but not limited to:

www.cnbc.com(CNBC)

Money.cnn.com (Money)

Finance.yahoo.com (Yahoo! Finance)

www.investors.com (Investor's Business Daily)

www.google.com/finance (Google finance)

www.cboe.com

CHOICE OF TRADE-OPTION
OR STRAIGHT STOCK?

When you decide to trade, and before you start trading, you need to do some homework and make a very important decision on which kind of trading you want to pursue? Do you want to trade straight stock? Or do you want to trade Options?

Whichever you choose to trade, whether stocks or options, your first objective is to make money. Number two objective is to make that money with the minimal acceptable risk because trading for a living is not that simple. It is a challenging job and the odds are against your success. But if you can master the 'skills', this will reward you in a way that no other job or career can.

Trading stocks and options online requires you to possess specific skills set like:

Risk Tolerance

be on alert always, reach a level of excellence, have a sound trading methodology that can thrive profitably in high volatility environment.

Risk Management

Brace risk management as your most important principle. I suggest you find a good trading school and get trained by the experts. Then you need to educate yourself seriously about everything you can about stock/options trading.

Find the best books on trading online and spend hours to learn and gain good knowledge and understanding of options trading. Some good books include but not limited to: "Understanding Option" by Michael Sincere 2nd edition. Options for the beginner and Beyond, by W. Edward Olmstead, 2nd edition. How to Make Money in Stocks by William O'Neal. You can also subscribe to his Investor's Business Daily. Trade Like A Stock Market Wizard, by Mark Minervini (U.S. Investing Champion). Trade Like Chuck (How to Create Income in Any Market), by Chuck Hughes. The list goes on! You can watch CNBC. I watch CNBC daily to follow up on market trend and social events that can impact the market. Watch and follow the conversations on: Squawk Box, the morning news and talk program where the notable people in business and politics discuss reports from Washington, Silicon Valley, London and the like. Squawk box benefits everybody, from the small investor to the professional trader. Mad Money and Daily Booyah by Jim Cramer is all about making you a more knowledgeable and intelligent investor by giving you options trade Strategies, best stock advice, and top stocks to buy. Fast Money, pre and post market show led by Melissa Lee and a round table of experienced traders like: Guy Adami, ("The Negotiator") Josh Brown ("Downtown" The Reformed Broker"), Jon Najarian, ("The Monster" "Dr Evil"), Pete Najarian ("The Pit Boss"), Karen Finerman, and Stephanie Link to name a few, bring important post market news to investors.

Open A Trading Account

Some good brokerage firms include but not limited to: E-trade, StockBrokers.com, T. D. Ameritrade, Trade Nations, Scott trade. E. Trade and Trade King are good platforms for a beginner. They charge reasonable commissions and execute orders fast. E–trade offers gateways to many global equities market should one want to trade any of them.

After you register with a broker, familiarize yourself with their set up and take advantage of their free trading tools and research. Depending on the broker you register with, you may have the opportunity to practice trading through a simulator. You can learn to set up trades, buy shares, and sell shares using paper trade simulator. When choosing a brokerage firm, consider the online brokerage firm that have knowledgeable customer service support who can help to guide you when placing trades and are willing to discuss option strategies. Bear in mind that it costs less to place your own trade, otherwise if the firm places the trade for you, consider the expense of the commissions.

CHAPTER 3

POINTS TO PONDER

Important points to consider when you are ready to start trading include but not limited to:

Qualities to Achieving the Goal

What is your goal, trading for a living?

It is important to have a goal in mind when trading or investing in stock market; and it is equally important to update your goal every so often.

When trading for a living, your goal is to maintain a consistent and reliable winning trades for profits to achieve financial freedom!

Emergency Fund

The first few months of your trading, you need to fortify your emotion for the profit inconsistencies that will follow.

You should have available in liquid fund at least one year's worth of cash in your account before you plunge into trading. This is the fund that you will apply towards your living expenses. This ready cash will give you peace of mind, prevent you from frustration and panic, and mitigate the anxiety that can develop during the following few months of your new career.

Remember your goal! FINANCIAL FREEDOM!!!

Cash Security

Secure your profits and do not turn it into failure during market corrections. Withdraw some profits you are making during bull market because it may not be readily available right away during market corrections. Years of bull markets can be followed by prolonged bear markets and increased volatility that can decrease your account value.

It is advisable to take your profit off the table when you achieve a financial goal. Do not run the risk of losing a significant portion of your savings. Although, it is a good thing to take some risk to reinvest your profits when the market is growing, but also, it is a wise thinking to realize that when you have enough cash to meet your specific needs, you should decrease investing or trading risk and protect your Hard–Earned profit. The first thing important to you is to meet your needs, once you achieve that take most of your cash off the table and protect it for peace of mind and easy sleep.

Emotion

Remember, when trading for a living, your goal is to maintain a consistent and reliable winning trades for profits to achieve that goal.

This will happen with time and patience. You require patience! Brace yourself to be able to endure the daily income fluctuations from your trading. You should not let your emotion overcome your good judgement. Keep your emotion at bay!

Winning Vs Loosing

Being human, you know, we want to win all of the time but this is not so in stock or option trading. Be aware that winning all the time is counterintuitive to our human nature. Brace your psych with this knowledge to prevent emotional upheaval. You cannot win all the time!

Naturally, stock/option trading is a combination of winning and losing. Sometimes, you lose more than you win. But the profit on your winning trades will wipe out the loses, wipe your tears and comfort you!

Discipline

The most important factor in trading is discipline! Cultivate discipline in your trading style to reduce risk. About 5 to 10 diversified trading positions will be adequate. Close out losing trades quickly to prevent huge loses and let your wining trades run for large profit. When it comes to Profit and Loss consider the risk involved. Know when to take profit. Do not hold tight to trades that are going south and losing money hoping that these trades will soon head northward. These trades may continue to decay with time and your money melting away.

Sell off the losing trades ASAP! Invest the remaining money you salvaged in other well researched stocks with "buy" signal. Maintain a healthy risk management that can yield you sizeable profit and keep it up.

Patience Is Golden

When you enter a winning trade, be patient! Do not scalp your profit. Allow your wining trades time to mature profitably upwards. One good wining trade can give you a meaningful profit that will make you laugh to the bank and wipe away your tears from your lost trades.

CHAPTER 4

OPTION TRADING CONCEPTS

Option trading is not stock trading. It is a good thing and highly recommended to be an educated option trader before beginning to trade. You can learn, design, and apply option strategies that will help you profit from a wide variety of stock market outcomes. You can accomplish this with little risk if you have the required knowledge of the fundamentals and the technical terms and meanings in financial markets.

Know your Fundamentals and Technical Analysis

Two schools of thought:

In financial markets, Fundamental and Technical Analysis are the two main schools of thought on the yardstick to measure a company's financial worth and management capabilities. Fundamental and technical analysis work together.

Fundamental Analysis

This school of thought looks at the company's fundamental economic factors. If the company has good fundamental strength, then the company's stock is a good opportunity to purchase. Therefore, before you buy shares of a company, use fundamental analysis to research and rate the company's financial stability to determine if you want to buy shares from that company, then wait and buy when the stock has come off base and trending up.

This is the process of analyzing the financial statements of the companies to be able to select quality stocks before you buy them. You use the data from the financial statements to compare with past and present data of the company and other companies within the same industry. By analyzing the data, the investor may arrive at a reasonable valuation(price) of the company's stock and determine if the stock is a good purchase or not.

Technical Analysis

This school of thought looks at the price movement of the stock and uses this data to predict its future price movements. It relies on reading charts, and stock graphs for specific stock patterns, and buying and selling signals.

In technical analysis, the investor can interpret the pulse of the market using different Kinds of technical charts. The investor will be able to analyze recent price patterns and current market trends to be able to predict future patterns and trends. Some patterns and trends can provide the technical trader certain cues or signals called technical 'indicators' about the future market movements. Some patterns with descriptive names like: "head and shoulder", "cup and handle," are considered a bullish trend and a buying opportunity. When these patterns begin to form, and traders recognize them, the technical trader can make investment decision based on the expected result of the pattern or trend. While Technical analysis deals with patterns, not performance. The patterns help the chartist to find price trends to determine upward or downward direction. Fundamental analysis on the other hand helps to decide what to buy and Technical signals when to buy it. Fundamental analyst will follow and study a company's financial performance for over a time period of say 3-5 years. If the company has been doing well, the analyst can safely recommend the company for a 'buy.'

To become an active or full–time trader, you have to grasp the fact that trading is a business that must generate consistent profits to sustain you and your family; one large loss may deplete your trading account so to master the skills set for trading stocks and options is very important.

Discipline

The most important factor in trading is discipline! Cultivate discipline in your trading style to reduce risk. About 5 to 10 diversified trading positions will be adequate. Close out losing trades quickly to prevent huge loses and let your wining trades run for large profit. When it comes to Profit and Loss consider the risk involved.

Know when to take profit. Do not hold tight to trades that are going south and losing money hoping that these trades will soon head northward. These trades may continue to decay with time and your money melting away.

Sell off the losing trades ASAP! Invest the remaining money you salvaged in other well researched stocks with "buy" signal. Maintain a healthy risk management that can yield you sizeable profit and keep it up.

Patience Is Golden

When you enter a winning trade, be patient! Do not scalp your profit. Allow your wining trades time to mature profitably upwards. One good wining trade can give you a meaningful profit that will make you laugh to the bank and wipe away your tears from your lost trades.

CHAPTER 5

MAKING MONEY WITH CALL OR PUT OPTIONS

Call Option

A call Option is a security that gives the owner the right to buy, for example, 100 shares of a stock or index at a certain price, known as "strike price" by a certain date known as the "expiration date." A call option is done when the market is going up and there is hope for huge profit. A call option has 4 arbiters: A call option will have an Underlying stock or index; Expiration date; A strike price; and the Right to buy the stock. The owner of a call option also has the right to "call the stock away" from the seller. Further, in a call option, even though he has the "right", he does not have the "obligation", to buy the stock (exercise the option) at the strike price if the stock falls in price and no longer profitable. The call owner can leave the option to expire worthless.

A call option has unlimited profit potential while the loss is only limited to the amount of premium paid on the stock. Note! Call option gives the right to buy.

Put Option

Put option gives the right to sell the stock in question. You buy put option when you anticipate the price of a stock or index to fall. Put option gives you the right to sell, for example, a 100 shares of stock or index at a certain price, known as "the strike price" by a certain date, known as the "expiration date". A put option has 4 character designs: There must be an underlying stock or index; It has to have an expiration date; It has a strike price; and must have "the right to SELL the stock in question at the strike price. It gives you the right to "put away", or sell, the said stock or index to another person. To compare and contrast put/call options: The Put option gives you the right to SELL, whereas the call option gives you the right to BUY the stock. You can buy put to make a profit when you think that a stock is going to fall in price soon because the stock price is too overpriced, or bad news is coming out, or the company will soon give their negative earnings report.

PROTECTION FROM POTENTIAL LOSS

Buying put is like buying insurance

A classic example when to buy put option is when Chipotle's stock dropped more than 10 points following bad news. On 7/21l2017 because it was reported and shown on the national television that a dead rat fell from their ceiling and live mice seen crawling on their floor. Chipotle stock dropped from $450 to $350 and continued to drop till the market closed. Yet another example, on 8/9/2017, PCLN Priceline Inc. dropped more than 165 points. In this scenario, if you buy 1put option contract of, the CMG at $450 and sell it at $350, you will profit at least $1000 less the premium you paid. Again, when CMG rebounds and starts going up again, you will be making money since you did not sell off your stock out of fear and panic during the downturn. This is how Put option helps to hedge your stock when the price is falling and makes you money from the price drop.

Put Protection

For peace of mind it is advisable to buy Put protection for your trades should share prices begin to decrease. Whether you are in Option or Stock trades, Put Option will give your trade positions protection/leverage and you can be rest assured that you will not incur losses when the market is going down. It is like buying life, home, or health insurance

Buying Put Protection(insurance) for your stock or option shares will give you peace of mind when stock prices begin to fall. It will limit your downward risk and enable you to increase your upward profit.

CHAPTER 6

BUYING SHARES TO MAKE A PROFIT

Do not buy stocks based on tips, hearsay or just because you love it. Bull market environment is a very ideal time for buying call options. Do your homework properly with Fundamental and Technical Analysis to research well to fish out underlying stocks with great potential to lift off.

When buying your shares consider the following:

Risk Management/ Entry Point

Trade options with the capital that you only allocate to speculation, not more than 10%. Do not trade options with the money you will use to pay living expenses like electric, gas auto, ins, auto finance, water, and the like. Do not trade option with the money for your kids education. Do not trade option with your safe money!

Better to sleep well at night by limiting your trading fund to the money that you can afford to bear the loss.

Entry Point

When stocks fall, you buy. When stocks go up, you sell. Purchase shares in increments! This is the buy low sell high phenomenon!

Pick the best stocks by applying your knowledge of technical and fundamental analysis.

To be able to pick the best stocks to buy, determine the company's financial situation by examining the company's earnings reports over time to find out the company's earnings per share (EPS) and the price earnings (P/E) ratio. EPS is very important to measure a company's profitability that is assigned to each share of stock. The price earnings ratio (P/E) tells how much investors can pay for every dollar the company earns in profit. Dividing the most recent share price by the most EPS will give the P/E ratio.

Making Your Stock Selection/Company Analysis

The following paragraphs will explain to you how to make your stock selection when you start trading option to generate income. Analyze the company from head to toe. To find out how well the company is thriving. Consider their:

1. Quarterly Earnings
Look at the company's current quarterly earnings per share should be up significantly like 25% to 50% more

than the same quarter the previous year. If the company has a small profit, it may report lower earnings the next quarter. Before you pick a stock compare the company's earnings per share (EPS) to the same quarter a year before. For example, compare the October quarter of this year to the October quarter of a year ago.

2. Annual Earning Increases

Take into consideration the Annual Earnings Increases of the company you want to buy their shares. This is supposed to show a promising growth every year for 3 years or more. This type of company stock will have very good chance for higher success to grow your income.

3. What about their Annual Return on Equity? Annual Return on Equity should be at least 17%. This will show you the difference between well-run company and the poorly managed. Annual cash flow per share should also be greater than actual earnings per share by at least 15%.

Stability and consistency of annual earnings growth for past 3 years should be considered when choosing a good company.

4. P/E Ratio:

Companies with poor management may offer low P/E ratio. Do not fall into this trap to buy their stocks thinking that the stocks are undervalued. According to William O'Neal, you can't buy a Mercedes for the price of a Chevrolet. Concentrate on stocks with proven record of significant earnings growth in each of the last 3 years plus strong recent quarterly improvements. (William O'Neal).

5. New products.

New products, services, change of management and new policy will have positive impact on the company's growth. For example, AMZN, AAPL, GOOGL always have new products in their pipelines: AMZN (fresh foods), GOOGL (driverless Cars), and AAPL (i-phone 8) to name a few. Supply and Demand of the stock play important part in choosing growth stocks. Short supply or over supply will impact the price of the products in one way or the other so choose the company wisely.

6. Time to Buy

Do not buy stocks just based on hearsay or just because you love the stock. Bull market environment is a very ideal time for buying call options. Do your homework properly with Fundamental and Technical Analysis to research well to fish out underlying stocks with great potential to lift off.

CAPITAL MANAGEMENT

Guard Your Capital.

Trade options with the capital that you only allocate to speculation, which should not be more than 10%. Do not trade options with the money you will use to pay for living expenses like utilities. electric, gas auto, ins, auto finance, water, and the like. Do not trade options with safe money or the money for your kids' education.

Better to sleep well at night by limiting your trading fund to the money that you can afford to bear the loss.

CHAPTER 7

OPTIONS VS STOCKS—WHICH IS BETTER?

I am an option trader. I prefer to trade option because it requires less capital than stock trading.

For example, to buy 100 stock shares of AAPL, I will pay about $9,800. But for one option contract which is equivalent to hundred shares, you will pay only about $1,300. I can buy more contracts and make more profits when the market is moving up and build up my capital. You can also trade option in your IRA Retirement Account. 100 shares of stock are equivalent to 1 option contract.

Option allows for a Reliable Back-Up Income. I started reading every book I could find on stocks and Options trading. I devoured all the books I laid my hands on, went to seminars, and webinars, and went to trade school, obtained certificate In stock and options trading before I became a pro trader. I was overwhelmed because everything seemed so complicated and confusing until I attended the trading school where I graduated and received a trading certificate. I decided to settle with options trading after learning the basic concepts.

Trading Option is super simple when you learn and apply the basic principles to "buy low" and "sell high" with some tweaks here and there on: emotion; discipline, and financial management.

No large capital is required like in stocks. You can make money quickly with little capital to trade options and you are almost certain of making money in any market condition up or down or sideways if the option strategies are applied appropriately when the opportunity presents. Consider the following basic option trading concepts.

DYNAMIC NATURE OF OPTIONS

Option trading can be used by traders to leverage assets and control some risks associated with trading. With option you can profit whether the stocks are going up, down, or sideway. You can use options to cut losses, protect gains, and buy large chunks of stock with little cash in your account. However, before you trade options, it is important to get the essential knowledge of option strategies and the effects the option variables like volatility and time decay will have on them.

BASIC CONCEPTS IN OPTION TRADING

Call Option–Gives you the right to buy something!

Put Option–Gives you the right to sell something! Therefore, the option contract gives you the right to buy or sell something (usually 100 shares of stock) known as the underlying asset or security; at a specific price, known as the strike price; for a specific period of time, from the option purchase date until the expiration date.

CHAPTER 8

TERMS IN OPTIONS MARKET

Option contract

1. One (1) option contract is equal to 100 shares of the underlying stock!

2. Exercising Rights–

Under an option contract, Mr. A can be said to be exercising his option rights when he buys or sells the underlying stock at the terms of the option contract.

Under an option contract, if Mr A sells an option to Mr. B and receives a cash credit, and if Mr. B wishes to exercise his rights to receive the stock from Mr. A, Mr. A has the obligation to deliver the stock at the strike price at which the option was sold.

If you buy an option, e.g. FB you are not obligated to buy the underlying stock for FB!

3. Option Premium–

Time value and intrinsic value make up option premium!

4. In-the-money–

When the strike price is below the stock price, or stock price is above the strike price, a call option is said to be In-the-money!

AT-the-money–

5. Out-of-the money–

In Out-of-the-money put option, the strike price is less than or below the current stock price.

6. Time Premium–

To assume the risk in price movement of an option, the writer of an option charges the buyer a dollar amount called Time Premium!

7. Time Decay-

The time value of an option decreases as the option expiration date gets closer!

8. Intrinsic Value–

Call Option

When a call option is in-the-money, the portion of the option's premium is the intrinsic value. Intrinsic value, used in option pricing, intrinsic value indicates the amount the option is in the money. Using face book stock for example, if the call option strike price for FB is $15 and the market price is $25, subtract 15 from 25 to will leave 10. This $10 is the intrinsic value of this face book call option. Therefore, intrinsic value is the difference between the market price of FB and the strike price.

Put Option

If a trader buys fb put option at the strike price of $20 and the market price is $16, the difference between $20 and $16, ($4), is the intrinsic value.

VOLATILITY

Volatility occurs daily from stocks and options trading activities. It is the statistical measure of the spread of returns on a given stock or index.

The prices of stocks are not constant, they move up and move down fluctuating by the seconds. The speed at which the prices change direction is known as volatility. The extent to which the prices deviate from the normal price can be calculated using standard deviation, the difference between returns from that same stock or market index.

The options trader will analyze this standard deviation to determine the extent to which the return of the stock will fluctuate from the purchase date to the date of the option's expiration.

While in a lower volatility, the value of the stock price

changes in a gradual steady pace over the time period. The option's trader in the market to buy and sell stocks options to make a profit will consider a stock with high volatility at a higher risk of return on investment knowing that due to high volatility the price of the stock can suddenly change up or down in a short period of time. There is a general belief that bearish markets are riskier than bullish markets.

Implied Volatility and Options

Implied volatility does not definitively predict what option price in the future will be. It only approximates what option price is likely to be in the future following the actions traders are taking with reference to the options which give the buyer the opportunity to buy or sell shares at a specific price during a predetermined period of time. It does not specify which direction in which the price change will go. Traders look at implied volatility when deciding which shares to buy. High volatility may signify price swing to very high or very low. Low volatility may show that price will not change drastically to either way soon but changes in value at a steady pace over a period of time.

Historical Volatility

Historical volatility measures past market activities, changes, and their actual results. Option traders consider historical volatility when dealing with an option, as this can sometimes be a predictive factor in the option's future price changes.

YOUR KNOWLEDGE IS YOUR POWER

Your experience and the skill of proficient option trading will not, and cannot be taken away from you once you garner them. This is a fair statement because you have personally been through the trials and tribulations during the course of your personal training in option education and practice. You have personally toiled and persevered to learn the ropes and nobody can take that plethora of information and skill of stock trading from you. 365 days in the year, plus minus the weekends, the ticker symbol is on in the stock market providing huge opportunities to determined traders and investors at the emergence of new companies in every industrial sector from retail stores, restaurants, medical equipment, Financial, and Technology, just to name a few.

Many years of persistent study and practice provided me with the necessary knowledge and the skills-set to achieve my goal to make my living in the stock option market.

CONFIDENCE AND HARD WORK

Persevere to succeed! Do not be discouraged by negative things some people will say to you. Some people may say that trading stocks and options is gambling and risky business. Some people may say to you "your cup is leaking, stop the leakage." This group of people are impatient, have no self-confidence, have no burning passion, no real commitment, think it is impossible to achieve success. They tried and failed. They failed because they did not dedicate the time and effort required to acquire the necessary education and skills set for this business.

TAKE RESPONSIBILITY FOR YOUR SUCCESS

As you take responsibility for your success, you will enjoy the freedom to be your own boss, to work at home, set your own schedule, do what you want when you want it. It is not easy to find any other business venture that can compare with trading stocks options. It is an undeniable fact that some people are gaining financial freedom and amassing wealth in the stock market. Be part of that! Stock market has huge opportunity with pride, but without prejudice for everybody.

CHAPTER 9

TRADING SYSTEMS

If you choose to trade options, there are trading systems like Vector Vest, Trade Nations, E-Trade, Barchart.com etc. that can help you achieve top performing growth and help you to invest or trade successfully. The systems can fish out long term winners, premier growth stocks and good dividend stocks. The systems can give you clear, easy to understand strategies and powerful tools and can quickly analyze the volume of stocks value, safety, and training and you will then with your sound stock/option trading education and the skills you learned from your readings and paper trading practice you will be able to decide on which shares to retain and the ones you can get rid of. You should consider the safety of the stock you plan to buy. Consider and apply the principles of stock analysis. You should know when it is time to buy a stock, sell it, or hold it.

Read every book you can find about options trading. If you have financial support I advise you to go to trading school for theory and practice paper trading before you embark on the real deal. The tools, techniques and strategies you will gather from the school and from reading voraciously from different books and from different authors will help you establish your trading plan and style. Being a master in your own readings will pay great dividends and save you from sleepless nights in your options trading marathon. Good luck!

FIND A GOOD BROKER

It is advisable to learn all you can about stocks and options trading before you dive Head on into trading.

Stock trading is buying shares/stocks of a Company at a low price with the hope to Sell the shares at a high price to make profit; or to make more money than you Initially invested. Be aware that:

Trading in stock market is risky but when done appropriately the profit potential is enormous.

Stocks are traded through stock exchanges (trading floors). There are stock exchanges throughout the world; some examples are: London stock exchange, NYSE, Shanghai stock exchange, Nigeria Stock Exchange and so many others. The exchanges bring the buyers and sellers of shares together. Most trades are done electronically through the marvels of technological efficiency and this method is more convenient and less hassle since computers handle all the trades. Physical trading floors are noisy and chaotic. BROKER!

It is better to elicit the help of a broker when you start trading stocks to save you time and money. Stock brokers are already registered members to most of the common stock exchanges. The registered stock broker will assist to buy stocks on your behalf for a small fee each time you buy and sell. Going through a broker saves you the trouble and the expense of registering to be a member of stock exchange yourself. For me, I use "E-trade" brokerage to buy and sell my shares.

What Is Option Trading?

An option is a written contract between the buyer and the seller. In this Written contract, the buyer is given the right, but not the obligation, to buy or sell shares at a specific price on or before a certain date. In the options market, the option contracts give the buyer the right, but under no obligation to buy or sell the shares or other assets at a predetermined price, within a predetermined time-period.

TYPES OF OPTIONS

Call and Put Options

With call option: you have the right to buy shares at a set price known as 'strike price.'

With put option: you have the right to sell shares to the option's writer at a set price.

Option contracts are quoted per share basis. Each contract is equal to 100 shares of the underlying stock.

Example: to buy call option on ABC stock that will expire in November, and the price is set at $2.50, I will spend $2.50 for each contract. The contract binds me to buy or sell the shares at any time before the expiration date in November.

Put Option Contract

gives the owner the right, but under no obligation, to sell a specific amount of underlying asset at a specified price and specified time duration. Option trading is more complicated than trading straight stock. It can be challenging for a beginner. That is why some traders begin by buying short-term calls especially out-of-the-money calls. Buying out-of-the-money (OTM) and at-the-money call ATM at the first glance is very attractive but it is not the best choice in placing trades. OTM is cheap and they follow a familiar pattern of buy low, sell high! In the out-of-the-money call, the trader must be sure of which direction the market is moving. The market will move 10% above the strike price in 30 days to be profitable, otherwise the trader incurs a loss. Buying in-the-money call which is more expensive will be profitable even if the market starts to fall.

Note: Call option 'right' to buy! Put option 'right' to sell! Both call and put options have no obligations!

CHAPTER 10

OPTION STRATEGIES

Option trading can be used by traders to leverage assets and control some risks associated with trading. With sound trading skill in option you can profit whether the stocks are going up, down, or sideway. You can use options to cut losses, protect gains, and buy large chunks of stock with little cash in your account. However, before you trade options, it is important to get the essential knowledge of option strategies and the effects the option variables like volatility and time decay will have on them.

1. Covered Call

In this strategy, you can own straight stock shares of a company and you can sell a call Option against those shares. For example if you hope that GE will increase in price, you can buy 100 to 500 shares of GE; you can sell a call against some of the shares because you already own the shares. In covered call strategy, if the market volatility is increasing you will incur a loss; but if the market volatility is decreasing you will make profit. If you choose and opt for straight stocks or options trading there are trading academies, Live Webinars that can train and coach you to become a pro on how to trade stocks and options. You should also read voraciously good books on stocks and options trading to gain wide knowledge and become a master in stocks and options trading.

2. Bull and Bear Spreads

In a bull spread strategy if you hope that the market will rise, you can buy a call on the shares you already own and at the same time sell a call on the same shares with the same month and expiration date but at a higher strike price.

In the Bear Put spread strategy, you buy a put on the shares you own and write a put on the same shares with the same expiration month but the strike price is lower. This strategy can help you make some money if used when you think that the market will fall, you use this bear put spread to capitalize on the decreasing price of the shares.

Stock trading, in this modern world, is within the reach of every Tom Dick and Harry made easy through the electronic system.

Option trading can be used by traders to leverage assets and control some risks associated with trading. With option you can profit whether the stocks are going up, down, or sideway. You can use options to cut losses, protect gains, and buy large chunks of stock with little cash in your account. However, before you trade options, it is important to get the essential knowledge of option strategies and the effects the option variables like volatility and time decay will have on them.

3. Married Put

An option trader can own or buy shares and at the same time buy put option equal to the number of shares on hand. A bullish trader hoping to make a profit when share price in upward trend will apply this Married Put Strategy to protect against any potential short-term losses like sudden fall in the call option share price. Married Put strategy is like buying an insurance policy to protect against unpredictable fall in price. When share price begins to fall the value of the put option will begin to rise.

4. Bull call Spread

In a bull call strategy, the trader is anticipating the price of the stock to rise. The trader will buy a call option at a given strike price and at the same time turn around and sell the same number of calls at a higher strike price. Both call options have the same expiration month and same underlying stock.

5. Bear Put Spread

In bear put spread, the trader will buy put options at a specific strike price and turn around sell the same number of puts at a lower strike price. Both options will have same expiration date and be the same kind of underlying stock. In this Bear Put Spread, the trader is anticipating the price of stock to fall. This strategy is another form of bull call spread. The trader is bearish and expects the underlying asset's price to decline.

CHAPTER 11

THE START OF STOCK TRADE

In the ancient world trade was by barter. The age of stock started in the late 16th century when the New World countries started to trade with each other.

Capital Requirement was unaffordable by one person, so groups of merchants got together and became partners and co-owners. These business partners formed joint stock companies with their shares which became exchangeable and a viable business model. The Dutch East India company issued the first exchangeable paper shares by which shareholders conveniently buy, sell and trade their stocks with other shareholders and investors. Shareholders and shares grew so fast and this led to the inception, beginning of organized marketplace where shares were exchanged by stockholders. Like the London Coffee House which stock traders took over in 1773 and changed the coffee house to "stock exchange"–This is how the first stock exchange, London Stock Exchange was founded. In 1790 a stock exchange was started in

Philadelphia. The wall street started in May 17, 1792 on the corner of wall street & Broadway, NY, under a tree where Buttonwood agreement was signed by group of 24 supply brokers inside 68 wall street in NY. In March,1817, the organization renamed the group the NYSB (New York Stock Board) then moved from the street into 40 wall street. Today, there are so many stock exchanges around the world making it easy for people to create personal wealth and financial stability, to create personal wealth and financial stability, allowing individuals to fund their retirement and other ventures through the stock market.

CHAPTER 12

MY NURSE WRAP

Why I chose to trade Option! Best business model!

Freedom! Freedom! Freedom!

Are you frustrated, angry, but pretending to save face and to feign the people pleaser. You are acting ethically even in the presence of risk? Are you burnt out or burning out, and feel stuck at your 9-5 jobs? Are you confused on what else you can do, how to do it, where to start, how to start? Relax for help is on the way! You have solutions! You can join the option traders! Become your own boss, earn more than double your income at the end of the day and secure your financial independence. Get a copy of this book: "Option Trade like Victoria!" Sure fire Income Generator informant! Read it and get the information you need to get your feet wet in the Stock Market with emphasis on Options Trading.

There are strategies to learn in option trading that will help you make money to live a better life and say "no" to burn out. High patient-to-nurse ratio, snobbish treatments from the management and all that baggage. I burned out in 2012; my body revolted. I experienced repeated health problems, 4 ambulance trips to the ER and panic attacks that made me look inside to search my soul and asked myself: from here going on, "What can I do? How can I do it? Where can I find help? and When should I do it?" I received a post card in the mail that invited me to dinner and listen to stock market pitch. After attending numerous seminars on stock market, I chose to study option trading in depth.

Option Trading saved my life! The strategies in options trading are instrumental in helping me make extra income when I switched to PRN shifts in my profession. If you are seeking the 'genuine' financial help, relax! There is a way out! I have been a Registered Nurse helping patients for more than 20 years.

Nurses are known as selfless givers who put others first giving their time and energy not minding their own needs with limited income, and underappreciated. Burnout is a threat to patient safety as depersonalization results in unpromising interactions with patients.

Nurses!!! are the pulse of the healthcare system! Florence Nightingale! In 19th century Florence Nightingale laid the foundations of professional nursing during the Crimean war. The Nightingale model of nursing education and her notes on nursing were popular. Florence Nightingale set up the first school of nursing, operating hospital connected to a medical school. This model of professional nursing education spread widely in Europe and North America after 1870. In the 1900s Nightingale model of nursing school started to fade away. Physicians and hospitals saw women in nursing as a source of free and inexpensive labor. Exploitation of nurses became common by employer, physicians and educational providers. Nursing was also considered a woman's profession while doctoring was considered a man's profession. Nursing became officially gender neutral late in 20th century, thanks to increased expectations of workplace equality.

According to (Bozell, 2004) in "why emotions matter." You can recruit till the cows come home, and that's what we see nurse recruiters in hospitals doing. Pull out all the stops, do the sign-on bonuses, basically bribe them in some way to get them in the door, but until you can stop the bleeding, they're coming in the front door and leaving out the back door."

Folks! You can join me in the Option platform. Learn how to trade stock options and become an option trader. Option trade will give you the opportunity to decrease your work load and work PRN till you discover firsthand the financial freedom in trading option. At first this may be difficult because you will learn the ropes of the trade. But it will become easy once you make up your mind to say 'no' to burnout. I have seen personally how option trading profit changed my life from 12-14 hour shifts and 12-14 patient ratio to becoming my own boss, making my own schedule and living better.

According to ANA (2002) the 4 major responses reported by nurses when asked why they left:

Exhausted, discouraged, saddened, powerless, frightened, are the emotions experienced by many nurses, myself inclusive, working the long hours. Because "I have been there and done that" I searched and wished to find another avenue for an alternative income to pay my bills and live life without the bustles and hustles in the hospital nursing life. I searched the stock option market and fell for option trade. My myriad of years of experience in option trading is given out for you in my book "Option Trade like Victoria." This book is written to invite the retired nurses, doctors, lawyers, unemployed everyday persons, stay home moms and pops, to join the world of Stock market with emphasis on option trading where the profit potential is huge and nobody will boss you around. Having traded options for many years and making more money than I made as a professional nurse I decided to pursue options trading full time. My urge to write this book, "Trade Options Like Victoria" (quick fire income generator) is to create a channel of information on stocks and options to inspire retired nurses, doctors, lawyers, the unemployed, the stay home moms and pops, and other interested everyday individuals, who want to achieve financial freedom but do not know that option trading exists and that it is REAL! Reading this book will help them to learn about option trading and to know option trading as another verifiable avenue for income.

"Options Trade like Victoria" should be a hub where nurses, retired, or practicing can connect to acquire option trading insights.

There is a popular belief that option trading is risky. But let me reiterate, living life itself daily is risky. Nothing is guaranteed and nobody knows what will happen tomorrow except the ALMIGHTY! Stock is risky! Option is risky too! Market movement is uncertain both for stock and option because when the standard fundamental analysis and technical analysis are overcome by emotions, this can negatively impact the market to sky high or bottoms up. Possible solutions to mitigate risk:

(1) master the skills set and master your emotions. (2) Adjust your trade positions by closing off losing trades;(3) Buy long calls or leaps by applying the straddle or strangle strategies; (4) Buy put options for protection; (5) Marry the stocks you are familiar with and keep speculation to a limit. (6) Know what to buy; when to buy; and when to sell! (7) Know these terms: Call, Put, Buy, and Sell.

Options trading has created many legendary option trading millionaires. In a similar way, option trading has left so many option traders with less money. losing all their money in no time. Using stock options together with stocks create opportunities that never existed before. When option trade is done appropriately, it can decrease your risk because unlike with stocks, you can put less money on the line.

When compared to the cost of the underlying stock options are very cheap. You can CONTROL same AMOUNT of stock for a fraction of the price.

For example, a trader might buy 100 shares of $80 stock. This trader will pay $8000 for the 100 shares. If the stock rises say 10% this trader makes only $800. But in option market, this trader can get in for less than $2 a share. When the stock rises, say 10% the value of the stock can go up to 1000%.

360 degrees TURN corner! FROM HOSPITAL FLOOR NURSING TO OPTION PLATFORM TRADING.

Yes! You heard me right. Nurse to Trader. Either way, I am still out to help people.

After many emergency trips to ER working 7pm to 7am with patient overload, I asked myself what my life would be going forward. Over the years I have garnered a portfolio of knowledge and expertise, which it would be good to impart to others.

My son approached me one day and said "Mom, I wish you and Dad will write your life history for us to keep."

I said to my son, yes, that's a brilliant idea! I have a dream in the stock option market which is unfolding and making sense, and should be put to book first. After discovering all the goodness and the money–making strategies in the stock option market, I became passionate and fell head over heel in this business. I developed a huge appetite for putting into writing my years of stock trading experience. Therefore, I would write this book to inspire and inform others that the stock option market offers the greatest opportunity in the whole world for verifiable income. It is the "Real Deal." The foundation of my writing is strengthened by the great works of stock option traders and investors. I have read numerous books and articles by great traders and investors, and attended many seminars and workshops on stock option trading, which gave strong foundation to my writing.

THE PATIENT DOG EATS THE FATTEST BONE!

Be patient! With the passage of time, your dedication and hard work, you will achieve financial independence.

To achieve a successful super income generating option business you have to know the tricks of the trade embedded in the option strategies. Read, learn, study, and be a master of the option strategies.

Learn and know the options skills-set and have them ready: What to buy; When to buy; and When to sell.

The option Mantra:

Call Option, Put Option, Buy, Sell.

What to buy! When to buy! When to sell!

APPENDIX

STOCK TRADE EVOLUTION

Joint Stock Companies

Stock trading, in this modern world, is within the reach of every Tom Dick and Harry made easy through the electronic system.

In the ancient world trade was by barter. The age of stock started in the late 16th century when the New World countries started to trade with each other.

Capital Requirement was unaffordable by an individual trader so groups of merchants got together and became partners and co-owners. These business partners formed joint stock companies with their shares which became exchangeable and a viable business model. The Dutch East India company issued the first exchangeable paper shares by which shareholders conveniently buy, sell and trade their stocks with other shareholders and investors. Shareholders and shares grew so fast and this led to the inception, beginning of organized marketplace where shares were exchanged by stockholders. Like the London Coffee House which stock traders took over in 1773 and changed the coffee house to "stock exchange"– This is how the first stock exchange, London Stock Exchange was founded. In 1790 a stock exchange was started in Philadelphia. The wall street started in May 17, 1792 on the corner of wall street & Broadway, NY, under a tree where Buttonwood agreement was signed by group of 24 supply brokers inside 68 wall street in NY. In March,1817, the organization renamed the group the NYSB (New York Stock Board) then moved from the street into 40 wall street. Today, there are so many stock exchanges around the world making it easy for people to create personal wealth and financial stability, allowing individuals to fund their retirement and other ventures through the stock market.

THE SUPPER STOCKS—CHART VIEW

December 5th to December 8th2017:
Amazon, Google, Facebook, Regeneron, & Tesla—5 days
chart view:
December 5TH to 8TH 2017.

Good upside day for AMZN, GOOGL, and FB. On December 8, AMZN traded up to $1170 while GOOGL was up $1155, and FB traded up to almost $182, while APPL continued to the downward slope.

REGENERON

Regeneron entered the week trading below $375 on Monday inching up to $385 by Tuesday. Traded lower than $370 on Wednesday, moved up to form the fanciful "W"on Thursday and Friday, then traded up seriously to above $380, and sideways by close of market on Friday December 8th.

AAPL

Apple entered the week trading lower–low to below $169 to Wednesday; moved sideways on Thursday; inched up to slightly over $170 before collapsing downward to below $170 by the close of market on Friday.

TESLA

Tesla entered the week trading down to below $302, then started upward trend to $370, moved sideways to consolidate on Tuesday, formed triple "M"; moved downward on Wednesday to above $302 before the serious uptrend on Thursday to $317. Formed the clear cut fanciful "W" between Thursday and Friday in readiness to move higher! The following week, Tesla proved the 'W' you right and continued to move higher to $342 and higher!

MEAN BUSINESS WITH YOUR TRADING

The internet has revolutionized the business process of making money and doing business online. Option trading is a business model that allows you personal and financial freedom.

For many years, I toiled successfully through the learning curve to study the variables in highs and lows of trying to make money online in option market. I have acquired enough personal experience to know what am talking about in my book. The main reason why many people do not achieve their objectives to make big money in the stock option market is that they act out of greed, fear, ignorance, and hope. They do not take the necessary time to study the characteristics and behavior patterns of great stocks like AMZN, GOOGL, FB, TSLA, & AAPL, to name a few. On the other hand, some who know the market lack the emotional discipline to wait for the winning trades to mature and finish unfolding upward. They do not treat their trading as a business should be treated. To be successful you should handle your option trading well, and treat it like a business. When you buy stocks, realize that those are your merchandise that you store in your portfolio. McDonald, Walmart, and Kroger, for example, store their business merchandise in their physical warehouse, and run day to day for profit. You see the similarity between your option trading business and the conventional Walmart, Kroger, and McDonald. You should therefore, run your option trading as a business to make profit. Buy shares that are leaders in the market so that you can sell them at a higher price. If you buy stocks that are laggards you will get stuck with them and you will eventually lose money, you may even lose your entire capital. Going through the learning curve studiously and patiently will pay you great dividend in the end. Get rid of the negatives in your thought process. Think big! Believe it in your mind that you can do it. You can!

If you have the right tools and attitude, you can be

successful in option trading without encountering high risk. But you have to be willing, and disciplined to allow yourself to learn the lessons in option trading.

If you are at the point in your life where you want to make a serious change like turning around 360 degrees, this book is for you. Buy it, read it to the end and act immediately to make your dreams for financial freedom come alive, and you will reap a huge dividend. Unlike other businesses or franchises that require large capital to start, you will realize that you will not need a lot of capital, 500–2000 may suffice to lift off your business. You will not worry about securing a physical store front and clamoring for good location. You will not order truck load of merchandise to store in the warehouse. In the same vein, no worries waiting to take delivery of the merchandise you ordered. Employee is out of the question! With Wi Fi internet connection anywhere across the globe, you can run your business. You will have the freedom, secured fulfilling job, peace of mind, and have more time to do things together with your loved ones. You can go on vacation, buy the things you want without financial constraint. Money will not be your problem but how to spend it!

SUMMARY

Victoria is a RN, the people helper, who discovered another financial pathway to help others who need help while focusing on their financial security and SAFETY. Just like Chuck Hughes, a former Air Force Pilot who trained to focus on SAFETY, he did not take a lot of money or risk to acquire great wealth, so is Victoria. Chuck's #1 goal is other people's financial security, so is Victoria's goal. As a financial mentor Chuck Hughes has helped others to make profit with ease and peace-of-mind. Chuck started his option business with $4,600 and made millions and continues to make millions. Victoria started her option business with trading penny stocks. Today she knows the option business strategies to teach others. Victoria's best day in this month of October 2017 was with Amazon, the day she took in a decent profit of $8,000 plus on record, without any loosing trade this quarter.

Option trade is a unique business that can allow you personal and financial freedom. Option may be your solution to 9-5 rat race. You can open your own business, operate it from anywhere with Wi Fi in the world, be your own boss, achieve financial and personal freedom without investing thousands of dollars.

If you are unemployed, want to quit the 9-5 grind, want to say goodbye to the long standing 12hour shifts, or you are just looking for an alternative avenue for extra income, you are welcome to the options trading platform! Technology platforms make the science of option trading much easier. Learning to trade option like a pro takes time and experience. Become passionate about becoming a top-notch option trader! Join option traders! You'll be glad you did.

BOOK DISCLAIMER!

STOCKS & OPTIONS INVOLVE RISK!

Investing in stocks and options involves risk, including possible loss of principal.

The information in this book is only educational and the author's opinion, and should not be construed as any kind of solicitation or investment recommendations. The author is not associated with any broker and not a registered investment advisor. Readers should seek professional advice from legal, registered representative before you plunge head on to trade stocks and options.

The author shall have no liability for any investment decisions based on the strategies or information provided in this book. Do not trade with the money you cannot afford to lose. Past profitable trades do not guarantee trades will be successful and profitable in the future.

Options and stock trading involve risks. Transactions are complex, carry a high degree of risk, and are not suitable for everyone.

The risk in trading can be substantial and you

may sustain a total loss of the funds that you invest if caution is not exercised. You should therefore consult a registered financial advisor, weigh your financial resources carefully, to determine if options and stock trading is suitable for you.

ACKNOWLEDGEMENTS

I made a powerful decision that transformed my emotional and financial life in 2004. Not knowing how powerful the result would be, this decision has allowed me to go from a life of stricken poverty to a life that gives me the opportunity to do what kind of business I want, with whom I want, when I want, and where I want. This decision was the catalyst for a business that has paid out priceless dividend–freedom! Freedom from the stressful 7 p.m. to 7 a.m. job. Freedom from conventional 9–5 job.

It will be your wise decision too, to buy this book and read it to completion. I have spent years going to seminars reading books, articles, and watching videos by expert traders to gather knowledge and experiences you will read about in this book. I could not have accomplished this on my own alone without the help of other people behind the scene. That said, I have a laundry list of people I owe gratitude. First person on my list to thank is my six years old daughter, Victoria Tobechi Angelica Okonkwo. In 2016, I had a ghastly car accident in which I was supposed to die. For the sake of my daughter, God defended me, dived in, and literally took the death away from me so that I might live to raise my daughter. My daughter, very brilliant, attends Olson Elementary School, Allen, Texas. To this day, my daughter and I sing "Living for Jesus" daily. My daughter has taught me not to give up in life. As a simple analogy, on daily basis, when I look for my pair of reading glasses or my car keys and don't find them, I will express frustration and quit. My daughter will look at my face and say to me, "Mommy! Take a deep breath, don't give up." "I'll help you find them." My daughter's ready intuitive advice is inspiring, encouraging, and motivating. In course of writing this book you are about to read, I encountered a road block, waiting indefinitely for E-Trade Brokerage to obtain permission for me to use some stock charts in my Portfolio for illustration in my book. I almost abandoned my book project but "mommy don't give up" replayed in my head, infused me with hope, energized, and motivated me to adjust and finish the book.

My Father was a great farmer. I inherited hard work, strength, and verbatim from him–tell it as it is! Speak the truth with authority kind of man. He worked with the pioneer priests from Europe fearlessly to establish Catholic Religion in my home town Enugwu-Ukwu, Anambra State, Nigeria.

My mother was a renowned market trader. My mother was very lovable and always beamed with smile. She taught me kindness, generosity, obedience, and truthfulness–"only the truth shall set you free" kind of woman.

Both my father and mother instilled in me the value of "God first", then business!

The credit and accolades should also go to my team behind the curtain: my son Osita for setting up the brokerage account. Albert for his computer support. Ruben for his technical support to the printer.

My thanks also go to Patience Odebiyi who expressed interest to help market this book.

I am thankful to my sisters "28" for their prayers for me.

Thank you, Chris, for helping to keep the dream alive and sometimes finding new challenges for me like "your cup is leaking."

I thank Ifeoma Okonkwo, Alex Okonkwo, and Angela Nworah for all the contributions they made towards the successful completion of this book.

INDEX

Printed in the United States
By Bookmasters